Fred Newton Scott

The principles of style

Topics and references with a prefatory essay

Fred Newton Scott

The principles of style
Topics and references with a prefatory essay

ISBN/EAN: 9783742865106

Manufactured in Europe, USA, Canada, Australia, Japa

Cover: Foto ©ninafisch / pixelio.de

Manufactured and distributed by brebook publishing software
(www.brebook.com)

Fred Newton Scott

The principles of style

TOPICS AND REFERENCES

WITH A

PREFATORY ESSAY

BY

FRED N. SCOTT, PH. D.

Assistant-Professor of Rhetoric in the University of Michigan

ANN ARBOR

REGISTER PUBLISHING COMPANY

The Inland Press

1890

PREFACE.

The contents of this pamphlet, with the exception of the Prefatory Essay, are taken from a note-book which the writer compiled for the benefit of his class in the Principles of Style. In the main, therefore, the references do not go beyond the resources of the University Library, though occasional note has been made of works which, it is hoped, the Library may soon possess. Books that are accessible to students of the University of Michigan are indicated in the Bibliographical Index by the affixed shelf number enclosed in brackets, thus [2. 7. 4. 5.]. The Prefatory Essay is not intended to be an original contribution to the theory of Style, but simply to make plain to other instructors who may care to use the references, the writer's purpose in compiling them.

FRED N. SCOTT.

ANN ARBOR, MICHIGAN, November, 1890.

CONTENTS.

CORRECTIONS.

Page 14, l. 6, *for* ecrite *read* écrite.

" 16, l. 20, *for* Microcosmos *read* Microcosmus.

" 19, l. 30, *for* student's *read* students.

" 20, l. 14, *for* problémes *read* problèmes.

" 22, l. 28, *for* rythm *read* rhythm.

" 23, l. 28, *for* Deutschen sprache *read* deutschen Sprache.

" 26, l. 5, *for* Prof. *read* Profs.

" 29, l. 20, *for* ecrivain *read* écrivain.

" 30, l. 19, *for* 30 *read* 27.

" 31, l. 3, *for* longeurs *read* longueurs.

PREFATORY ESSAY.

If we use the term Rhetoric in its broadest sense to mean the principles and practice of literary effect, there are three ways in which the subject may be profitably studied. The student may, in the first place, try to get from the reading of a text-book practical instruction in writing essays. That is, he may commit to memory rules and hints to be applied in the construction of 'compositions'—artificial things .ich ͠enerally sustain to the real things he will be .lled upon to produce in after life,— letters, editorials, sermons, harangues, stories, sketches, and occasionally essays properly so-called — the same relation that five-finger exercises sustain to symphonies and sonatas. These practical helps he will find given him by the text-books in the form, generally, of abstract and arbitrary rules—"Thou shalt" do this or avoid that. The reasons for the rule may or may not be given, but in either case the student is not at a stage to profit much by them. The rule in all its bareness and blatant practicality is exactly what he needs and about all he is likely to get. "Short sentences should follow long ones," "Particular terms are more forcible than general terms"—a few dogmas of this

Three ways of studying Rhetoric.

1. As a guide to composition.

Abstract rules.

sort must be worked into the student's raw and wincing memory by main strength and the habit of using them reduced to automatism long before, in most cases, the student can have more than a vague glimmering of the reasons that underlie them. This does not mean that the Rhetoric or the instructor should conceal the truth that every rule has a reason back of it. On the contrary, that fact cannot be too often dinned in the student's ears. He will not be able, probably, to recall very much about the reason and what he thinks he recalls will be absurdly wrong; but some day he will remember that there *is* a reason and perhaps be curious to know something about it. If that stage ever comes, or is brought about by artificial means, then the student is prepared to profit by a second method of studying rhetoric.

Search for a principle. This consists in a search for some fundamental principle, the various special applications of which furnish the rational explanation of the rules before mentioned. I say 'search' because, although the illuminating principle itself is usually flaring at the very entrance of the book, the student rarely takes it with him in his exploration of the interior. As a general thing it is not until he has accepted any number of corollaries as fundamental and unrelated principles that he begins to suspect the existence of a larger principle from which the corollaries are derived. The verification of this suspicion and the discovery that the larger principle is that annoying formula which the instructor has been harping on ever since the first lesson was assigned, mark a decided advance in intellectual development. Henceforth, some interest, it may be expected, will be shown in the subject not only for its utility as a guide to practical composition, but for its value as an organized system of facts worth knowing. In short, the study of Rhetoric as a science is now fairly begun. It need not be inferred, however, because the scientific interest increases, that the practical value of the study must at the same time diminish. Rather, practical applications are now unfolded in terms which the student, in his unenlightened state, could not be expected to understand. "Follow the order which corresponds to the self-movement of the subject." Admirable! But a student will have torn his palms on division, definition, amplification and the like for months, before he sets foot on that good eminence. So with the instructions, such as can be given, for the adjustment of matters of sentential stress and rhythm, and for the internal structure of the paragraph. So with the whole question of the order of precedence of the various kinds of subordinate clauses.

2. Science of Rhetoric.

New meanings in old words.

At this stage, rhetorical instruction, it is generally held, reaches its limit. At any rate, if it goes beyond this point it ceases to be a science. It passes the knife-edge boundary which a carefully-worded definition will nicely set about

Ultima Thule.

each individual department of knowledge, and it henceforward wanders distracted in the melancholy and dim land of Aesthetics

> Quivi sospiri, pianti, ed alti guai
> Resonavan per l'aer senza stelle.

Or if haply it flies shrieking from this limbo of Lost Ideas, it may be unlucky enough to get over into the adjoining territory of Literature among dramas, epics, novels and other

> Gorgons, and hydras, and chimaeras dire.

"Step over this line" says the rhetoric-maker, scratching in the accumulated dust of ages, "and you get into the region of the vague. Rhetoric cannot account for the finer effects of literature. There is an indescribable bloom, a charm"—and so on. We all believe in the indescribable bloom and charm, though it must be confessed the formula is getting rather tiresome; but is it true that any exact line of division can be drawn between the vague and the definite? To the average student, everything is vague at first. The bloom that goes with the

substitution of a particular for a general term is to his mind not less indescribable than is the dying fall of a line of Keats to the presumably more piercing intelligence of the instructor. After a time, if he is diligent, the student memorizes a reason for this particular kind of bloom, and later, if he is fortunate, he gets some idea of what the reason means. He goes on in this way from beginning to end of his study, at every step clearing up vaguenesses and learning to describe blooms and charms. This process comes to an end, not, in most cases, because the truly Indescribable blocks the way, but because the last page of the Rhetoric has been recited and review has begun. *The tether of the text-book.* The acquisition of ever clearer knowledge might go on for a life-time, and in very many cases, let us hope, it actually does so. Of course a text-book must end somewhere and have at least a semblance of completeness and finality or it will be unfavorably reviewed by the journals. Suppose then, we call the kind of rhetoric commonly taught from text-books in our High Schools and Universities, the Lower Rhetoric (not meaning thereby to depreciate it but simply to give it a convenient handle), and suppose again that we embrace all further incursions into the vague and all further strivings to describe blooms and charms, under the name of Higher Rhetoric.

3. The Higher Rhetoric.

Now the student, as he passes from the Lower to the Higher treatment, while he will not be made aware of any absolute breach of continuity between the two, will yet feel a growing sense of otherness. For one thing, he will find that his instruction calls for the exercise of certain mental functions in higher degree than was formerly the case. Imagination and Feeling, which had little employment while the Lower Rhetoric was in progress, are now required at every step. The student is not argued with so much as appealed to to feel as his instructor does, or frankly to differ with him. If he respond tardily to the appeal, his advancement is slow and hesitating. Further, just as when he entered upon the study of the Science of Rhetoric, he must learn a new vocabulary, or rather learn to attach new meanings to old words and phrases. But what meaning? That is something he cannot learn from the dictionary. He must come to feel the thing itself before he can feel any value in the symbol of the thing. And almost his only hope, if the feeling hangs fire, is to read, to read: to go through crises of wild, blind enthusiasm for the worst passages of Macaulay, Scott and Ruskin; to linger in sickly sentimentality over syrupy lines of Rossetti and Swinburne; to explode with admiration at bad metaphors in Dickens, Lowell and Holmes. If the good passages can be admired, so much the better; but unless there is sincere love or hate for something the work had better be abandoned.

Appeal to Feeling.

Cultivation of a sense for literary values.

One aim of the Higher Rhetoric then is the cultivation of a sense for values in literature, but if we consider carefully we shall see that this is only one phase of a more general process, namely, an advance toward concreteness, —concreteness in all the student's conceptions. Some vague feeling of rightness there must have been at the very beginning of the study, else the student could not have applied even the simplest precept. What is being accomplished now is the emancipation of this feeling, giving

Return to nature.

it a chance to grow out from under the memor-
ized abstract rule, to grow away from it appar-
ently at first, but really, as will later turn out to
be the case, to grow into it and give it meaning
and vitality. All the new sap of feeling and
imagination that collects with the study of
the Higher Rhetoric, should flow back into
the hard abstractions of the Lower to give
them richness and ease. The student's practice—his paragraphing, the management of
the rhythm of his prose, even his cap-
italizing, spelling and punctuation—ought to
come more easily and naturally to him through
this infusion of life into dry bones. And as for
the grasp of principles, he will probably come
to wonder whether, before, he ever had hold of
any principles at all, so vividly does he now
realize for the first time that whatever is not a
piece of his own personality can be nothing but
an ɛἴδωλον—a paste-board box to hold abstractions.

Abstractions made concrete.

Shadows, not substantial things.

A piece of his own personality!—that, after
all, is, in the Higher Rhetoric, the only kind of
goods worth having. If we say cultivation of
taste, what should we mean but holding on
steadfastly and sincerely to what takes hold on
us—satisfies, that is, what of personality we
have achieved up to that point in our development—and striving to grow in grace and knowledge so that more things may take hold on us?
Or if we say that a writer must obey the Laws
of Composition, what should we mean but that

Growth of personality.

he is to make these laws a part of his own personality and then utter himself? Or if finally we say that such and such compositions are masterpieces of style, what can or ought we to mean but that they are the perfect expression of personalities worth expressing?

The Secret of Style.

To develop this rational and sensitive personality is, then, the object of the Higher Rhetoric, no matter whether the student's aim be to produce good literature, to appreciate that produced by others, or simply to learn the laws and principles of good writing. To that end three lines of progress will converge: the cultivation of a sense for literary values by wide reading, the study of Rhetoric as a science, and the union of feeling and knowledge through practice. And in practice I would include not composition alone, but the equally indispensable discipline of criticism, provided only the criticism be not mere notes of appreciation or mere compilation of statistics—both are good in their way—but an earnest attempt to get at the rational element of what we feel to be good.

Feeling and Reason united by Practice in Composition and in Criticism.

The object of the course for which this reference-book has been prepared, is to furnish the student with all legitimate help on his way to a better understanding of the Higher Rhetoric. The course has been called the Principles of Style, because Style is a word which, when used in its broadest sense and not as the complement of Invention, comes near to summing up those

Object of the course.

concrete elements of good literature with which the Higher Rhetoric is concerned. The method of instruction might, of course, be varied infinitely, but the topics and references here given have been arranged to accord with the following programme:

1. *Lectures* of a suggestive character designed to relate the familiar rules of the Lower Rhetoric to some of the primary facts of Logic, Psychology and Aesthetics, and to a lay a more philosophical foundation for the student's own investigations. Among the topics which call for this treatment may be mentioned, the Definition and Kinds of Literature, the Relations of Prose and Poetry, the Nature of Language, etc.

Programme of the Course: 1. Lectures.

2. *Personal research* of three kinds:

2. Personal research.

(a) The examination of essays in criticism to discover upon what basis famous critics have founded their judgments of literature. This has been found profitable on three accounts: it is interesting work; it brings the student into personal relations with an excellent class of literature; it presents him with the principle in a concrete form. The results of the research may be presented to the class in the form of papers or verbal reports and the value of the principles form the subject of a general discussion.

(b) The reading of special treatises upon style. The selection of the treatises must of course depend largely on the number of hours that the course occupies and the more or less elementary character of the work. The main object is to get out of the groove of the regular text-book, to see, for example, what Spencer himself said about Style instead of taking upon trust what some third person thinks he ought to have said. ·The results of this investigation may also be presented in brief papers or verbal reports and should, if possible, be vigorously discussed by the class.

(c) Essays on special topics. Each member of the class may be assigned a particular topic to work up into a thesis, the latter to be of greater or less length according to the grade of work that is being done and the time devoted to the course.

3. Study of Specimens of Style. 3. *Study of specimens of style* to verify the principles. For class-room purposes Saintsbury's Specimens of English Prose Style or Genung's Handbook of Rhetorical Analysis will exactly answer the purpose. Prose selections are of course to be preferred for the more elementary work. Genung's Handbook contains valuable suggestions for methods of instruction, but, as in all other things, the instructor must here hew out his own method. If the members of the class can be encouraged to read through the works from which the selections are taken, so much the better.

Arrangement of the references. The material which follows has been arranged in the order: (a) References to accompany the lectures; (b) Specimen critiques; (c) Topics for individual research; (d) Bibliographical index.

The lists are intended to be suggestive merely, and in consequence, no high degree of comprehensiveness has been aimed at. As not all the works mentioned are, very obviously, of the same degree of abstruseness, some pains has been taken to discriminate between them by means of brief commentaries or characterizations, which, it is hoped, will not be mistaken for critical judgments. A few suggestions have been added for the benefit of more advanced students.

Two classes of topics have been discriminated, although one naturally passes into the other: (a) Those of an elementary and more or less technical character, demanding little more than patience and accuracy, but yet affording a discipline not without its value; (b) Those requiring considerable exercise of independent thinking. The number may be increased indefinitely by substituting other authors, increasing or narrowing the scope of the field of inquiry, etc.

TOPICS AND REFERENCES.

i. ORIENTATION.

Certain fundamental questions concerning the relations of Style to other facts of knowledge are sure to arise at the very beginning of the course, and, unless at once disposed of, to recur at intervals in an increasingly annoying aspect. The approach to them will be easy if the student has had a thorough grounding in Psychology, but they can be satisfactorily answered only in the light of some elementary principles of Philology and Aesthetics; and although these principles, as before suggested, are to be given by lecture, the instruction may profitably be supplemented by outside reading in some of the following references.

1. DEFINITION AND CLASSIFICATION OF LITERATURE.

MATTHEW ARNOLD. Discourses in America.*

P. 72-137 Literature and Science. See p. 90 for a distinction between Literature and Belles-lettres.

BROOKE. English Literature.

P. 1 Definition of Literature.

BURT. Some Relations between Philosophy and Literature.

CARLYLE. On Heroes.

See p. 151 for a characterization of Literature.

DE QUINCEY. Works.

For De Quincey's distinction between the Literature of Knowledge and the Literature of Power, see his essay on Pope and Letter III of his Letters to a Young Man.

---

* For full bibliography and shelf number to this, as to all other references, see Bibliographical Index.

DOWDEN.   Transcripts and Studies.

See p. 237-240 of the essay on the Interpretation of Literature.

GAUCKLER.   Le Beau.

P. 178-182. Gauckler's term for Literature in general is *L'art de la Parole*, which he considers under three heads: *La Poesie, L'art oratoire* and *La Prose ecrite.*

HUNT.   Studies in Literature and Style.

See p. 7 for definition of Literature.

LAURIE.   Lectures on Language.

P. 81-104.

LEWES.   Principles of Success in Literature.

P. 1-23.

MORLEY AND TYLER.   Manual.

P. 1.

JOHN MORLEY.   On the Study of Literature.

See p. 38-39 for several definitions of Literature, p. 40 for Morley's own definition.

JOHN MORLEY.   Voltaire.

A definition and characterization of Literature will be found on p. 13-15.

NETTLESHIP.   The Moral Influence of Literature.

NEWMAN.   The Idea of a University.

P. 268-294.

POSNETT.   Comparative Literature.

Chap. 1.

STE. BEUVE.   Causeries de Lundi.

V. 3, p. 38-55 Definition of a Classic.

SCHERR.   Allgemeine Geschichte der Literatur.

V. 1, p. 1-2.

TAINE.   History of Literature.

Introduction.

THIRLWALL.   Essays, Speeches and Sermons.

P. 284-311. The present State of Relations between Science and Literature.

BASCOM.   Philosophy of English Literature.

VINET.   Outlines of Philosophy and Literature.

P. 457-481.

BAGEHOT.   Literary Studies.

A plea for the introduction of the term *literatesque* to mean what is available for purposes of literary art, will be found in Vol. 2, p. 341.

NOTES.

ARNOLD. For Arnold's lecture, if duplicates are needed, see 19th C. 12:216, Pop. Sci. Mo. 21:737. The lecture by Huxley to which Arnold's lecture is in part an answer, may be found in Nature 22:545 or Pop. Sci. Mo. 18:159. Huxley touches on the same theme, but with somewhat more liberality toward letters, in his Liverpool lecture, an abstract of which is published in Nature 27:396. The lecture in full appeared in Lond. Jl. Educa., March, 1883. See also Brackett's Relation of Modern Science to Literature in Pop. Sci. Mo. 15:166. Arnold's essay in Macm. 19:304 on the Modern Element in Literature has at the beginning a few paragraphs on the Nature of Literature.

MORLEY. Morley's lecture on the Study of Literature was reprinted in the Critic 7:169.

STE. BEUVE. The definition of a classic will be found translated in Morley's Study of Literature, p. 38-39.

Of the references given above, ARNOLD, DE QUINCEY, JOHN MORLEY, NETTLESHIP, NEWMAN AND THIRLWALL, are best adapted for assigned readings of a popular character. BROOKE, HUNT, MORLEY and TYLER, CARLYLE and STE. BEUVE, contain each only a paragraph or two bearing directly on the topic. BURT, GAUCKLER, VINET and SCHERR are philosophical though not violently so; TAINE and POSNETT scientific. LAURIE and LEWES are not concerned so much with defining literature as the one in pointing out its educational value and the other the conditions necessary to the successful pursuit of literature as a profession.

For advanced students, more technical and profound treatments of the subject may be sought in Gerber's Die Sprache als Kunst, V. 1, p. 43-122, Paul's Grundriss d. Germ. Philol., Methodenlehre, p. 216, *et seq.*, Hegel's Aes-

2

thetik, V. 3, p. 220-282. The relation of literature to the other arts is a profitable line of research.

2. RELATIONS OF THOUGHT AND LANGUAGE.

ENCYCL. BRIT. 9th ed. "Philology" by W. D. Whitney.
See esp. p. 766, *et seq.*

WHITNEY. Language and the Study of Language.
P. 403-420.

WHITNEY. Life and Growth of Language.
P. 1-31.

PAUL. Principles of Language.
Esp. Introd. and p. 1-19.

DEWEY. Psychology.
P. 3, 211-213.

SULLY. Outlines of Psychology.
P. 337-351.

PEILE. Philology.
Chap. 8.

HAMILTON. Lectures on Metaphysics and Logic.
P. 98-99, 432-439.

LOTZE. Microcosmos.
Vol. 1, p. 618-639.

JAMES. Psychology.
Vol. 1, p. 236, 241, 245, 251-261-283.

VICTOR EGGER. La Parole Intérieure.

BRUCHMANN, K. Psychol. Studien.
II Teil.

BALLET. La Parole Intérieure.

WEIL. Order of Words.

MAX MUELLER. The Science of Thought.

MAX MUELLER. On the Science of Thought.
See esp. p. 34-61.

EARLE. Philology of the English Tongue.
See Chap. 5 on Symbolic and Presentive Words.

LEWES. Problems of Life and Mind. 3d Ser.
See Problem 4, Chap. 5, for a comparison of words to Algebraic Symbols.

D. J. HILL. Science of Rhetoric.
P. 19-32.

REV. PHILOS. 22:1 De la parole. Stricker.

NOTES.

MAX MUELLER. For further discussion of Mueller's theory see 19th Cent. 23:569, 743; Nature 36:249, 37:323, 364, 412; Contemp. 54:475, 806; Princeton Rev. 1881 (Vol. 1) p. 108. The same subject is also briefly treated by Romanes in his Mental Evolution in Man, p. 81–83.

The best works for popular reading are doubtless WHIT-NEY, PEILE and EARLE. The article in the Encyclopædia Britannica is more concise and harder for most students to comprehend. The work of Max Mueller first mentioned is rather bewildering to the non-philological student, but the second, a book made up of letters published in the Open Court, is of a more popular character. Of the psychologies, DEWEY is brief but very suggestive; SULLY more detailed; JAMES a mine of valuable information for those who are sufficiently advanced to appreciate him. PAUL is admirable, but requires considerable familiarity with the terminology and history of Philology. HAMIL-TON'S forcible illustrations make his explanations clear for most readers. The chapter in LOTZE is for those who have done considerable philosophical reading. VICTOR EGGER and WEIL are pieces of brilliant research, one dealing with the relation of the word to the thought, the other with the relation of the order of words to the order of thoughts.

3. POETRY AND PROSE.

BAIN. On Teaching English.
Chap. 7.

ENCYCL. BRIT. 9th ed. 'Poetry' by T. Watts.
See esp. p. 261-262.

COLERIDGE. Complete Works. Vol. 4.

The famous statement of the antithesis of poetry and science occurs in Vol. 4 in the introductory essay on Definition of Poetry. See also pages 387-388 on the Wonderfulness of Prose.

ABBOTT AND SEELEY. English Lessons.

See p. 54-104, 145-151.

MASSON. Essays.

See p. 447-475 on Prose and Verse.

PATER. Appreciations.

P. 1-13.

SAINTSBURY. Specimens of English Prose Style.

In the Introduction Saintsbury has some curious reflections on the metrical movement of prose.

POSNETT. Comparative Literature.

See p. 49-52 and the foot-note on p. 51-52.

BASCOM. Aesthetics.

See the opening paragraph of Chap. 7.

VINET. Outlines of Philosophy and Literature.

See p. 544 and the paragraph on Rhythmical Unity, p. 492.

GENUNG. Practical Rhetoric.

See p. 48-84 for contrasts of poetic and prose diction.

GUMMERE. Hand-book of Poetics.

P. 84, 157.

WALTER. Lessing on Poetry and Painting.

P. 5-9.

SPENCER. Philosophy of Style.

In § iv Spencer attempts an explanation of the Superiority of Poetry to Prose.

MASSON. De Quincey (Engl. Men of L.).

See p. 190-198 on De Quincey's Prose-poetry.

D. J. HILL. Science of Rhetoric.

P. 33-37.

CONTEMP. 47: 548 On Style in Literature. R. L. Stevenson.

P. 552-556.

WHATELY. Elements of Rhetoric.

Part III, Ch. 3, § 3-4.

DE QUINCEY. Essay on Rhetoric.

In the next paragraph to the last of this essay, Whately's distinction of poetry from prose is ingeniously criticised. See also De Quincey's note.

DE QUINCEY. Essay on Style.

In discussing, in Part II, the probable origin of prose, De Quincey points out some important distinctions between prose and poetry.

GUYAU. Problèmes de l'esthétique contemporaine.

See p. 175-177.

SHAIRP. Aspects of Poetry.

Ch. 14-15 Prose Poets.

HUNT. English Prose.

Part II, Chap. 2.

NOTES.

An attempt to set down the names of all who have written on the theory of poetry would result in a *progressus ad infinitum.* For a moderately long list of such, see Gayley and Scott's Guide to the Literature of Aesthetics, p. 76, *et seq.* For the present purpose only those have been selected who touch upon the relations of poetry to prose. Of these, WATTS (Encycl. Brit.) is undoubtedly the most penetrating. MASSON'S essay on Prose and Verse should be read in the light of the essay on poetry that follows it. PATER and STEVENSON treat the subject briefly, but skillfully. BAIN, ABBOTT and SEELEY, GENUNG, and D. J. HILL, are more interested in the formal aspects of the problem. COLERIDGE must be read for his historical importance. In the other cases the discussion is too brief to require comment, though all are well worth reading.

For advanced student's Vischer's Aesthetik, Vol. 3, p. 1205-1211, may be recommended for thoroughness and profundity. Hegel's attitude on the subject, if one may judge from current quotations, has been generally misunderstood. The sections of the Aesthetik on the differences of prose and poetry, Vol. 3, p. 220–282, should be known at first hand. Most of the systematic German treatises on Poetics, as those of Viehoff, Wackernagel, Gottschall, Kleinpaul, and Wilh. Scherer. either throw light on the question or succeed in making the darkness visible.

4. Rhythm and Metre.

Spencer.   First Principles.

Chapter on Rhythm.

Kawczynski.   Essai comparatif sur l'origine et l'histoire des rythmes.

Helmholtz.   Sensations of Tone.

Hauptmann.   The Nature of Harmony and Metre.

Charles Henry.   Rapporteur Esthétique..

Guyau.   Problémes de l'esthétique contemporaine.

P. 178-223. See especially p. 178-182 on the Rhythm of Language and its Origin.

Gummere.   Poetics.

Part III Metre.

Sully.   Outlines of Psychology.

Dewey.   Psychology.

P. 58-68, 185-187 Rhythm.

Genung.   Practical Rhetoric.

See p. 169-171 for the Rhythm of Prose.

Minto.   Manual of English Prose Literature.

P. 24.

T. A. Arnold.   Manual of English Literature.

See the Appendix on English Metres.

Mod. Lang. Notes, 4:97.   Certain considerations touching the Structure of English Verse.   W. H. Browne.

Sylvester.   The Laws of Verse.

Lanier.   Science of English Verse.

Abbott and Seeley.   English Lessons.

P. 145-221.

EVERETT. A System of English Versification.

RUSKIN. Elements of English Prosody.

FORTN. 22:767. The Blank Verse of Milton. J. A. Symonds.

, SYMONDS. Sketches and Studies in Italy.
On Blank Verse.

MAYOR. English Metres.

JENKIN. Papers, Literary, etc.
See Vol. 1, p. 149-170, for a theory of Rhythm in English Verse.

GUEST. History of English Rhythms.

SCHIPPER. Englische Metrik.

CONTEMP. 47:548. On Style in Literature. R. L. Stevenson.
See p. 552-556 on the Rhythm of the Phrase.

✗SPENCER. Philosophy of Style.
See § iv, in which Spencer offers an explanation of the effect of rhythm in
poetry.

DUEHR. Ueber Metrik und Rhythmik.

GURNEY. Power of Sound.
Chap. 7, and Chap. 19 on The Sound Element in Verse. See also appendix D.

ENCYCL. BRIT. 9th ed. 'Poetry' by T. Watts.

DE MILLE. Elements of Rhetoric.
P. 276-282.

BAIN. Rhetoric.
P. 285-294.

MARSH. Lectures on the English Language.
Lect. xxiv Accentuation.

SCHMIDT. Introduction to Rhythmic and Metric.

BULWER. Caxtoniana.
Rhythm of Prose.

GRAY. Works.
Vol. I, p. 322-386.

REV. PHILOS. 28:356 Le Contraste, le Rhythme, la
Mesure. Ch. Henry.

NOTES.

Some notion of the general character of rhythm and the part it plays in nature may be gained from the chapter in SPENCER, which no one will have any difficulty in understanding. The psychology of rhythm is treated by DEWEY and SULLY. HELMHOLTZ, the great authority on musical rhythm as on all other matters pertaining to tones, is formidable both for bulk and for complexity. HAUPTMANN is of truly German profundity, not to be understood without great travail of spirit, but well worth the labor. HENRY has made some curious discoveries with regard to the psycho-physical aspects of rhythm and their mathematical equivalents. GURNEY is a storehouse of interesting information and always intelligible.

On the vexed subject of metre, the standard works are GUEST, LANIER, MAYOR and SCHIPPER. GUMMERE is intended for class-room use, but embodies the latest scientific research. T. A. ARNOLD, ABBOTT and SEELEY are useful brief compends. SYLVESTER is a conglomerate of translation, comment and digression, but contains a few interesting observations on metre from a mathematical point of view, obscured by a preposterous terminology. The articles by BROWNE (Mod. Lang. Notes), JENKIN, and SYMONDS are adapted to the needs of the non-technical student. A statement of the controversy over the various theories of metre may be found in the opening chapter of MAYOR.

The rythm of prose is a subject that still awaits careful investigation. GENUNG and MINTO contain useful hints from the practical stand-point. A few pages full of suggestion are to be found in GUYAU, who is always readable, and a very deft handling of the subject in STEVENSON'S essay on Style (Contemp.) Advanced students should consult Aristotle's Rhetoric, III, 8, and Cope's Introduction, p. 303.

Further references will be found in the Guide to the Literature of Aesthetics, p. 101. See also prefaces to first and second editions of Gummere's Poetics.

5. TONE–COLOR AND HARMONY.

GUMMERE. Poetics.

See p. 160-164 on the Qualities and Combinations of Sounds, and see index under *alliteration, rhyme, assonance.*

CAMPBELL. Philosophy of Rhetoric.

Some of the more obvious uses of qualities of sound are pointed out by Dr. Campbell in the Section entitled Words Considered as Sounds, p. 327-342.

GENUNG. Practical Rhetoric.

P. 61-62, 168-169.

LONGRIDGE. The Formation of English writers.

See Part 2, Chap. 1-2.

CONTEMP. 47:548. On Style in Literature. R. L. Stevenson.

See p. 557-560 for remarks on alliteration and assonance in prose.

GUYAU. Problèmes de l'esthétique contemporaine.

P. 224-243 La Rime riche.

SPENCER. Philosophy of Style.

See § lv for Spencer's rationale of rhyme.

BLAIR. Lectures on Rhetoric and Belles Lettres.

Lecture xiii On Harmony.

GRABOW. Ueber Musik in der Deutschen sprache.

DUEHR. Ueber Metrik and Rhythmik.

KAMES. Elements of Criticism.

Ch. 18

DE MILLE. Elements of Rhetoric.

P. 265-276

LANIER. Science of English Verse.

Part III The Colors of English Verse.

WHATELY.   Elements of Rhetoric.
Part III, Ch. 2, § 5 Words Considered as Sounds.
BAIN.   Rhetoric.
P. 110–120.
MARSH.   Lectures on the English Language.
See Lects. xxiii-xxv on Rhyme, Alliteration and Assonance.
CONDILLAC.   Oeuvres.
Vol. 7, p. 429 Dissertation sur l'harmonie du Style.

NOTES.

Most of the systematic treatises referred to under Metre and Rhythm have something to say also about the qualitative value of words and word-combinations, but no very satisfactory treatment of the subject is as yet available. The best, LANIER'S, is hurried and desultory. LONGRIDGE has brought together most of the traditional (and fanciful) ideas upon the emotional value of consonant-combinations and long and short vowels. CAMPBELL, KAMES and BLAIR are mostly concerned with the concord of sound and sense. The student will find in them the well-worn examples retained in most modern text-books. GUMMERE'S treatment is brief but meaty. SPENCER'S theory of the physiological effect of rhyme and rhythm has been generally adopted. See, however, the note on p. 441 of Gurney's Power of Sound. The *Schulprogramme* of DUEHR and GRABOW are excellent, especially that of the latter, which is a special investigation into the musical elements of German speech. Some interesting notes on the character of rhyme-words in English will be found in Prof. A. S. Cook's article on English Rimes, Mod. Lang. Notes 3: 209.

6. FIGURES.

GUMMERE. Poetics.

Gummere distinguishes between Tropes and Figures and makes the two
together the equivalent of style. See p. 83-132.

KAMES. Elements of Criticism.

Ch. 20.

BLAIR. Lectures on Rhetoric and Belles Lettres.

Lectures xiv-xviii.

CAMPBELL. Philosophy of Rhetoric.

Book III, Chap. 1.

MINTO. Manual of English Prose Literature.

P. 11-14.

D. J. HILL. Science of Rhetoric.

P. 203-243.

GENUNG. Practical Rhetoric.

P. 85-107.

BIESE. Das Metaphorische in der dichterischen Phantasie.

SPENCER. Philosophy of Style.

See § ii on The Effect of Figurative Language.

MOD. LANG. NOTES 3:251. The Evolution of Figures
of Speech. J. P. Fruit.

WHATELY. Elements of Rhetoric.

Part III, Ch. 2, § 2-3.

BAIN. Rhetoric.

Part I, Chap. 1.

MOD. LANG. NOTES, 1:140. The Classification of Rhetorical Figures. C. B. Bradley.

LORD. Characteristics and Laws of Figurative Language.

NOTES.

While much good ink has been spilled in discussing the
proper classification of Figures, little light has been thrown
on their origin or the principle of their effectiveness.
SPENCER'S lead in making Figures an outgrowth of the

principle of economy, has been pretty generally followed, in particular by GENUNG and D. J. HILL. GUMMERE'S research into the historical relations of Metaphor and Simile may be found in his thesis on The Anglo-Saxon Metaphor. The articles in Mod. Lang. Notes by Prof. Bradley and Fruit will be found suggestive.

7. THE LOGICAL STRUCTURE.

RENTON.   Logic of Style.
Chap. III Of Quantity.

WHATELY.   Elements of Rhetoric.
Part I.

BAIN.   Rhetoric.
Part I, Ch. 5.

MINTO.   Manual of English Prose Literature.
P. 3-11.

CAMPBELL.   Philosophy of Rhetoric.
Book III, Chap. 5, § 2 on the manner of using the Connectives in combining Sentences.

GENUNG.   Practical Rhetoric.
P. 176-179, 193-214, 245-248.

CONTEMP.   47:548.   On Style in Literature.   R. L. Stevenson.
P. 549-553 The Web.

PATER.   Appreciations.
See the remarks on logical coherence on p. 18-21

NOTES.

It would be easy to multiply references under this head, since almost every rhetoric has something to say about sentential or paragraph structure, or about the logical procedures of Invention so-called. The ablest handling of the subject is that of RENTON, which few undergraduate readers are prepared to understand. GENUNG'S treatment of the paragraph is in every way admirable.

8. Definition of Style.

For this topic see the references on p. 29. The most famous definition is that which Buffon narrowly escaped making—*Le style est l'homme même*. What Buffon actually said, is, it appears, *Le style est de l'homme même*, but it may be questioned whether he would have meant anything different had he used the words commonly attributed to him. On this point see Mod. Lang. Notes 5:179–180. Striking definitions of style will be found in Lewes's Principles of Success in Literature, Chap. vi; Pater's Appreciations, p. 33–35; Fortn. 25:244; De Quincey's Essay on Language, last four paragraphs; Joubert's Pensées, Vol. 2, p. 273; Renton's Logic of Style, p. 56; Coleridge, Complete works 4:337. See also the discussion in Mod. Lang. Notes 3:29, 113.

ii. CRITIQUES.

The object which the student should set before him in examining these critiques is to discover (1) What are the elements or qualities of style that the critics have thought it worth while to consider, (2) What principles have they advanced, if any, to sustain their judgments of praise or blame.

1. COLVIN. Landor. [Engl. Men of Letters].
   Chap. 9.
2. COLVIN. Selections from Landor.
   Preface.
3. TROLLOPE. Thackeray. [Eng. M. of L.].
   Chap. 9.
4. SAINTSBURY. Dryden. [Eng. M. of L.].
   Chap. 9.
5. VENABLES. John Bunyan. [Great Writers].
   Chap. 9.

6. STEPHEN. Johnson. [Eng. M. of L.].
Chap. 6.

7. WARNER. W. Irving. [Am. M. of L.].
Chap. 10.

8. COURTHOPE. Addison. [Eng. M. of L.].
Chap. 9.

9. TRAILL. Sterne. [Eng. M. of L.].
Chap. 10.

10. JOHNSON. Lives of the Poets.
(a) Dryden, (b) Pope, (c) Milton, (d) Cowley, (e) Waller, (f) Addison, (g) Swift.

11. MORISON. Macaulay. [Eng. M. of L].
Chap. 2.

12. GOSSE. From Shakespeare to Pope.
(a) P. 1-36 Poetry: the Death of Shakespeare, (b) p. 155-189, The Reaction.

13. STEDMAN. Poets of America.
See references in the Index under 'Style.'

14. STEDMAN. Victorian Poets.
(a) Chap. 2, (b) Chap. 3, (c) Chap. 4, (d) Chap. 5, (e) Chap. 9.

15. STEPHEN. Hours in a Library. First Series.
Essay on De Quincey.

16. MASSON. De Quincey. [Eng. M. of L.].
Chap. 11.

17. MATTHEW ARNOLD. Mixed Essays.
P. 180-204 A Guide to English Literature.

18. SWINBURNE. Essays and Studies.
P. 123-183 Matthew Arnold's New Poems.

19. BAGEHOT. Literary Studies.
Vol. 2 Essay on Gibbon, p. 31-53.

20. MORLEY. Burke. [Eng. M. of L.].
Chap. 10.

21. NICHOL. Byron. [Eng. M. of L.].
Chap. 11.

22. STEVENSON. Men and Books.
P. 91-128 Walt Whitman.

23. BURKE. Select Works.
Vol. 1. Introduction by E. J. Payne.

24. FORTN. 25:494 Macaulay. J. Morley.
25. PATER. Appreciations.
(a) Wordsworth, (b) Lamb, (c) Browne.
26. FRASER. 55:249. Literary Style. W. Forsyth.

iii. TREATISES ON STYLE.

1. ESSAYS.

LEWES. Principles of Success in Literature.
SPENCER. Philosophy of Style.
BUFFON. Discours sur le Style.
DE QUINCEY. Essay on Style and Essay on Rhetoric.
COLERIDGE. Complete Works.
Vol. 4. p. 337–343, On Style.
PATER. Appreciations.
Essay on Style.
CONTEMP. 47:548. Style. R. L. Stevenson.
See the same article in Critic, 6: 189, 199, 213.
HIGGINSON. Atlantic Essays.
P. 23–47, Literature as an Art.
JOUBERT. Pensées.
Vol. 2, p. 273–300 Du Style, p. 301–341 Des Qualités de l'ecrivain.
LONG. An Old Man's Thoughts.
P. 92–101 Style.
MINTO. Manual of English Prose Literature.
Introduction.
NEWMAN. The Idea of a University.
Lecture on Literature.
RENTON. The Logic of Style.
SAINTSBURY. Specimens of English Prose Style.
Introductory Essay.
FORTN. 25:243. Modern English Prose. G. Saintsbury.
ROYAL IRISH ACAD. TRANS. 5:39–92. On Style in Writing. R. Burrowes.

DRAKE. Essays .... illustrative of the Tatler, Spectator and Guardian.

Vol. 2, p. 1-116 On the Progress and Merits of English Style.

MACM. 37:78. Style. T. H. Wright.

The same article may be found in Pop. Sci. Mo. 12: 340.

HIGGINSON. Hints on Writing and Speech-making.

BULWER. Caxtoniana.

SCHOPENHAUER. Sæmmtliche Werke.

V. 6, p. 536-581, Ueber Schrift-stellerei und Stil.

ZEITSCH. F. VOELKERPSYCHOL. 4:465. Zur Stylistik. H. Steinthal.

STEDMAN. Victorian Poets.

Introduction.

HUNT. English Prose.

Part II.

NOTES.

BUFFON's discourse should be read by all because of its historical importance. His definition of style has already been spoken of, p. 30. What does he mean by it, and why does he prefer general to particular terms?

Everyone should know SPENCER at first hand, and in the same connection should be read the article by WRIGHT (Macm. 37:78). WRIGHT offers a justification of SPENCER's somewhat startling conclusions concerning the ideal stylist. See also Gurney's Power of Sound, p. 441 note. LEWES, who is admirably clear, vigorous and comprehensive, has availed himself of SPENCER's theory of Economy, but offers a criticism of it at the beginning of the section on Sequence. LEWES's three principles of Vision, Sincerity and Beauty are easily grasped by students and frequently stick in their memories when other and more conventional precepts leave no trace.

DE QUINCEY's long and rambling essay on Style and his

shorter essay on Rhetoric have been so rifled by rhetoric-makers that they seem, like Hamlet, full of stale quotations. The student may skip, with profit, the *longeurs* on Isocrates and the Athenian orators, in the essay on Style. Renton is probably right in saying that DE QUINCEY marks an epoch in the history of Rhetoric second in importance to that made by Aristotle, and is equally just when he says further that DE QUINCEY's contribution would have been much greater had his philosophical basis been sounder.

LONG has nothing particularly new to say, but says it with a charming garrulity. DRAKE deals mainly with Addison and Addisonianism. JOUBERT is a string of verbal brilliants not less meaningful than brilliant. NEWMAN's Lecture on Literature restates delightfully some of the simple truths of the text-books. SAINTSBURY's Introduction is mainly historical, showing the evolution of modern sentence- and paragraph-structure. It contains interesting remarks on prose rhythm. His article in Fortn. 25:243 briefly outlines the principles of style, then criticises Froude, Swinburne, J. R. Green and others. HIGGINSON's essays are for young men with literary aspirations. That on Literature as an Art is excellent. The essay by BURROWES in the Royal Irish Acad. Trans. is old-fashioned but not without merit.

RENTON's book is probably the best thing in existence on the Logic of Style, but the author's fondness for logical subtleties and obscure semi-humorous metaphors makes it, for beginners, unnecessarily hard and dark.

The Introduction to MINTO's Manual is sometimes used as a text-book and taken in connection with the rest of the work, it should answer that purpose well, as far as it goes. The author does not make much effort, however,—perhaps

4

that did not lie within his purpose—to help the student
out of the conventional ruts.

The most important recent contributions of a popular
character to the theory of Style, are the essays of STEVEN-
SON (Contemp. 47) and PATER. The former is mostly
concerned with technical points. The latter works from
a philosophical basis. In connection with STEVENSON
should be read ARCHER'S essay in CRITIC, Vol. 8. Flaubert's Letters will be asked for by those who read PATER.

A few paragraphs on style with a comment on Buffon's
definition (misquoted) will be found in Stephen's Hours
in a Library, 2d series, p. 201. Brockhaus's Conver-
sations-Lexicon contains a brief but suggestive article
on "Stil," mostly taken from Rumohr. Milton's comparison of poetry and rhetoric, often quoted (or rather misquoted) as a canon of style, will be found in his Tractate
on Education. See the use made of it by STEDMAN in the
Introduction to his Victorian Poets. Chap. 18 of Hosmer's
History of German Literature discusses German Style
interestingly. Ruskin and Arnold, the first in Vol. 3 of
Modern Painters, the second in his essays on Translating
Homer, have touched on the characters of the "grand
style." See, for these references, Cook's Touchstones of
Poetry, which contains also Ruskin's rules from Fiction,
Fair and Foul. Bourget writes subtilely on style in his
essays on Flaubert and the brothers de Goncourt, in Essais
de Psychol., pp. 156–173, and Nouveaux Essais, pp. 180–
198. Wordsworth's Prefaces are of interest in the discussion of poetic diction.

Of the older English treatises, it is perhaps unnecessary
to do more than mention Jonson's Discoveries, Sidney's
Apologie for Poetrie, Webbe's Discourse, Puttenham's Art

of Poesie, Constable's Reflections on Accuracy of Style, and Pope's Essay on Criticism. The list might be extended indefinitely, but would be of value only to the specialist.

The advanced student may consult, for artistic style in general, Veron's Aesthetics, references under Style in the index; Vischer's Aesthetik, references under Styl, Stylgegensatz, Stylgesetz and Stylisirung; Von Hartmann's Aesthetik, Vol. 2, references under Stil. On literary style especially, see Richter's Aesthetik, Vol. 2, p. 601–656, the article by STEINTHAL in the Zeitsch. f. Völkerps. 4:465, and SCHOPENHAUER'S treatise referred to above.

Those who are taking up the historical development of stylistic theory will wish to consult most of the following works: Aristotle's Poetics; The Treatise on the Sublime by Longinus; Horace's Ars Poetica; Cicero's De Inventione Rhetorica, De Oratore, Brutus, Orator, Topica and De Partitione Oratoria; Quintilian's Institutes; Dante's De vulgari eloquio; Bembo's Le prose; Vida's De Arte poetica; Boileau's L'Art poétique, and Voltaire's article on Style in the Encyclopædia (Oeuvres, Vol. 20).

2. RHETORICS.

ARISTOTLE. Rhetoric.

QUINTILIAN. Institutes.

HOBBES. English Works.

> V. 6, p. 513, The Art of Rhetoric. The preceding portion of the Whole Art of Rhetoric, p. 428-512, is an abridgment of Aristotle.

CAMPBELL. Philosophy of Rhetoric.

KAMES. Elements of Criticism.

BLAIR. Lectures on Rhetoric and Belles Lettres.

WHATELY. Elements of Rhetoric.

BAIN. Composition and Rhetoric.

A. S. HILL.   Principles of Rhetoric.
D. J. HILL.   Science of Rhetoric.
GENUNG.   Practical Rhetoric.
BASCOM.   Philosophy of Rhetoric.

NOTES.

The above list is designed to point out for the student a few systematic treatises on Rhetoric which are important for their historical influence, for their breadth of treatment, or for both reasons together. ARISTOTLE is, of course, the first great authority. Changes in modes of life, thought, and verbal communication have done little to destroy the practical value of his precepts, while for an understanding of the theory he is simply indispensable. The difficulty of understanding the Rhetoric is commonly overrated. Most of it is intelligible even to beginners. The English trio, CAMPBELL, KAMES and BLAIR, are much talked about, but little read. As practical guides they point the way to that 'proper' kind of style which is elegantly impersonal and sickeningly correct, but as repositories of information upon special topics they will amply repay frequent consultation if not consecutive perusal. CAMPBELL is undoubtedly the most sensible and original of the three. The student's reading of them will be far more profitable if he first gets some notion of the philosophical and psychological tenets of the Scottish School. On Kames in particular see Schasler's Kritische Geschichte der Aesthetik, Vol. 1, p. 295. For special students Cope's Introduction to Aristotle's Rhetoric, Spengel's Studium der Rhetorik bei den Alten, and Volkmann's Rhetorik der Griechen und Römer will be found of great critical value. See also the closing chapter of Vischer's Aesthetik and the brief essay by Schopenhauer in The World as Will and Idea, Vol. 3.

iv. TOPICS FOR PERSONAL RESEARCH.

1. TECHNICAL.

1. Analysis of paragraph-structure.
See Genung's Practical Rhetoric, p. 193-219.
- (a) Macaulay.
- (b) Dryden.
- (c) Sir Philip Sidney.
- (d) Lamb.
- (e) Gibbon.
- (f) Locke.
- (g) Spencer.
- (h) Burke.
- (i) Freeman.
- (j) Froude.

2. Character of the sentential cadence.
See Genung's Practical Rhetoric, p. 171, Longridge's English Writers, Part 2, p. 17-18.
- (a) Macaulay.
- (b) Ruskin.
- (c) Thackeray.
- (d) Milton.

5. Proportion of words of Saxon to words of Latin derivation.
- (a) Macaulay.
- (b) Johnson.
- (c) Bunyan.
- (d) More.
- (e) Dryden.
- (f) Matthew Arnold.

6. Use of *will* and *shall, would* and *should.*
See White's Words and their Uses, p. 265; Head's Shall and Will.
[2. 12, 1. 5.]
   (a) Bunyan.
   (b) Lamb.
   (c) Goldsmith.
   (d) Addison.

7. Use of alliteration and assonance in prose.
See Contemp. 47:556-561.
   (a) Macaulay.
   (b) Ruskin.
   (c) Thackeray.
   (d) Milton.
   (e) Sir Thomas Browne.
   (f.) Carlyle.
   (g) Newman.
   (h) Pater.

8. Archaisms and the use made of them.
   (a) Lamb.
   (b) Helps.

9. Newly-coined words and the use made of them.
   (a) Carlyle.
   (b) Lowell.
   (c) Dickens.

10. Examples of poetic diction in prose writing.
See Genung's Practical Rhetoric, p. 48-76. Abbott and Seeley's English
   Lessons, p. 54-104.
   (a) Burke.
   (b) Carlyle.
   (c) Hawthorne.
   (d) Ruskin.

11. Cases of inverted order and reasons for them.
   See Genung's Practical Rhetoric, p. 60, 165-169.
   - (a) Ruskin.
   - (b) Thackeray.
   - (c) De Quincey.
   - (d) Dickens.
   - (e) Scott.

12. Irrelevant clauses.
   Genung's Practical Rhetoric, p. 176-178. Minto's Manual, p. 10. D. J. Hill's Science of Rhetoric, p. 195-196.

13. Devices for showing the connection between sentences.
   Genung's Practical Rhetoric, p. 198-207.
   - (a) Carlyle.
   - (b) Newman.
   - (c) De Quincey.

14. Devices for showing the connection between paragraphs.
   - (a) Macaulay.
   - (b) De Quincey.

15. Classification and statistics of the various kinds of figures employed.
   See preceding references on figures.
   - (a) Burke.
   - (b) Johnson.
   - (c) George Eliot.

16. Sources of similitudes.
   See Minto's Manual, p. 56-58.
   - (a) Lamb.
   - (b) Lowell.
   - (c) Scott.
   - (d) Hazlitt.

17. Discrimination of synonyms employed.
  (a) Arnold.
  (b) De Quincey.
  (c) Sir Thomas Browne.

18. Violations of 'parallel construction.'
  See Genung's Practical Rhetoric, p. 208.
  (a) Boswell.
  (b) Froude.
  (c) J. R. Green.

19. Methods and devices of description.
  See Genung's Practical Rhetoric, p. 328–353.
  (a) Ruskin.
  (b) Dickens.
  (c) Howells.
  (d) Bulwer.

20. Examples of melody and harmony, and means by which the effects are secured.
  See preceding references on tone-color and harmony, and appendix to Bain's Rhetoric.
  (a) Hawthorne.
  (b) Burroughs.
  (c) Irving.
  (d) Pater.

21. Examples of harshness and explanation of this effect.
  (a) Locke.
  (b) Bacon.
  (c) Dryden.
  (d) Browning.
  (e) George Meredith.

22. Rewrite paragraphs from (a) Macaulay and (b) Emerson combining the short sentences into longer ones.

23. Rewrite passages from Bunyan, substituting modern

phraseology and using a larger proportion of Latinisms.

24. Rewrite paragraphs of Gibbon that describe trivial scenes or events, modifying the rhythm and language to suit the subject.

25. Turn passages of William Morris into the vernacular.

26. Figures of fancy and figures of imagination.

See Dewey's Psychology, p. 195-196, Ruskin's Modern Painters, Vol. 2, p. 137-204.

(a) Dickens.

(b) Lowell.

(c) Holmes.

27. Arrangement of dynamic stress.

See Genung's Practical Rhetoric, p. 181-184.

(a) Morley.

(b) Motley.

(c) Landor.

28. Reasons for order of subordinate clauses.

See Spencer's Philosophy of Style, Lewes's Principles of Success, Chap. III.

(a) George Eliot.

(b) Webster.

(c) Stevenson.

(d) Huxley.

 2. For More Advanced Work.

1. Value of 'adaptation' as a fundamental principle of Rhetoric.

See Mod. Lang. Notes, 5: 209-211, Campbell's Philosophy of Rhetoric, Book 1, Chap. 1, Genung's Practical Rhetoric, p. 1. See preceding references on Rhetoric.

2. Classification of figures.

See preceding references on figures.

3. Value of the distinction between figures and tropes.

3. Origin and psychological explanation of figurative language.

5

4. Meaning of Buffon's definition of Style.

Mod. Lang. Notes, 5:179–180, Saintsbury's French Literature.

5. Thackeray's Esmond as an imitation of the style of the time portrayed.

6. Teutonisms in Carlyle.

7. Comparison of Latin and English sentence-structure and rhythm.

See Weil's Order of Words.

8. Characteristics of Shakespeare's prose.

9. Value of the principle of Economy as the fundamental principle of Style.

See preceding references on Style.

10. General changes in the scope and character of Rhetoric due to (a) the invention of printing, (b) the rise in importance of the newspaper.

11. Relation of Rhetoric to Logic and Aesthetics.

BIBLIOGRAPHICAL INDEX.

[Shelf numbers are enclosed in brackets. V. is used for Volume and P. for Page in foreign as well as in English works. See English Men of Letters for books in that series.]

Abbott, E. A., and Seeley, J. R. English Lessons for English People. Boston: 1872. [2. 12. 3. 4.]

Adams, J. Q. Lectures on Rhetoric and Oratory. [2. 12. 3. 4.]

Archer, W. See Critic.

Aristotle. De Arte Poetica, [Vahlen's Text] with Trans. by E. R. Wharton. Oxford: 1883. [2. 7. 3. 7.]

―――― The Rhetoric. Trans. ... by J. E. C. Welldon. Lond: 1886. [Catal. R.]

Arnold, M. Discourses in America. Lond: 1885. [2. 7. 5. 4.]

Arnold, M. Essays in Criticism. Boston: 1869. [2. 7. 5. 4.]

Arnold, T. A. A Manual of English Literature, historical and critical. With an appendix on English metres. Am. Ed. Rev. Boston: 1882. [2. 7. 3. 5.]

Bagehot, W. Literary Studies. Ed. by R. H. Hutton. 2 v. Lond: 1879. [2. 7. 4. 5.]

Bain, Alex. On Teaching English. With detailed examples, and an Enquiry into the Definition of Poetry. Lond: 1887. [2. 12. 3. 4.]

―――― English Composition and Rhetoric. N. Y.: 1871. [2. 12. 3. 4.]

Ballet. Le Langage Intérieur. Paris: 1886.

Bascom, J. Aesthetics; or, the Science of Beauty. N. Y: 1886.

────── Philosophy of Rhetoric. N. Y.

Biese, A. Das Metaphorische in der dichterischen Phantasie. Berlin: 1889.

Blair, H. Lectures on Rhetoric and Belles Lettres. Phila: 1886. [2. 12. 3. 4.]

Boileau-Déspreaux, N. Oeuvres Complètes. ... Publ. par P. Chéron. Paris: 1875. [3. 6. 5. 3.]

Bourget, P. Essais de Psychologie Contemporaine. 4e. ed. Paris: 1885. [3. 7. 5. 6.]

────── Nouveaux Essais de Psychologie Contemporaine. Paris: 1886. [3. 7. 5. 6.]

Brooke, S. A. English Literature. [Lit. Primers.] New ed. Lond: 1878. [2. 7. 3. 5.]

Bruchmann, K. Psychologische Studien zur Sprachgeschichte. Leipzig: 1888.

Buffon, G. L. L., Comte de. Discours sur le Style, suivi d'extraits choisis. Notes d'Antoine Rondelet. Paris: 1883.

Bulwer. Caxtoniana. Lond: 1863.

Burt, B. C. Some Relations between Philosophy and Literature. Univ. of Mich. Philos. Papers, No. 4.

Carlyle, Th. On Heroes, Hero-Worship and the Heroic. N. Y: 1846. [2. 8. 5. 3.]

Coleridge, S. T. Complete Works. Ed. by Prof. Shedd. 7v. N. Y: 1853-4. [2. 9. 3. 3.]

Colvin, S. Selections from the Writings of W. S. Landor. Lond: 1882. [2. 9. 2. 5.]

Condillac, E. B. Oeuvres. 10v. Paris: 1798. [3. 14. 5. 4.]

Constable, J. Reflections upon Accuracy of Style. Lond: 1734. [2. 12. 3. 5.]

Contemp. 47:548. On Style in Literature. R. L. Stevenson. [Same art. in Critic 6:189, 199, 213.]

Cook, A. S. The Touchstones of Poetry. Selected from the Writings of Matthew Arnold and John Ruskin; with Introd. by A. S. Cook. San Fran: 1889. [2. 7. 4. 8.]

Cope, E. M. An Introduction to Aristotle's Rhetoric. Lond: 1867. [3. 3. 3. 6.]

Critic 8:7, 19, 57. R. L. Stevenson: His Style and Thought. W. Archer.

De Mille, J. Elements of Rhetoric. N. Y: 1878. [2. 12. 3. 4.]

De Quincey, Thos. The Collected Writings. New and Enlgd. ed. by D. Masson. Lond: 1890. [2. 9. 1. 6.]

Dewey, J. Psychology. N. Y: 1890.

Drake, N. Essays, Biographical, Critical and Historical ... illustrative of the Tatler, Spectator and Guardian. 2d. ed. Lond: 1814. [2. 9. 4. 4.]

Egger, V. La Parole Intérieure. Paris: 1881.

Encycl. Brit. 9th. ed. 'Poetry' by Th. Watts.

———— 'Philology' by W. D. Whitney.

English Men of Letters:

Colvin, S. Landor. [2. 9. 2. 5.]
Courthope, W. J. Addison. [2. 10. 2. 7.]
Masson, D. De Quincey. [2. 9. 1. 6.]
Morison, J. C. Macaulay. [2. 7. 4. 4.]
Morley, J. Burke. [2. 9. 5. 5.]
Nichol, J. Byron. [2. 9. 1. 5.]
Saintsbury, G. Dryden. [2. 10. 1. 7.]
Stephen, L. Johnson. [2. 10. 1. 4.]
Traill, H. D. Sterne. [2. 10. 1. 3.]
Trollope, A. Thackeray. [2. 8. 3. 4.]

Flaubert, G.   Correspondance.   Paris: 1887.

———— Lettres à G. Sand.   Paris: 1884.

Fortn.   25: 234.   Modern English Prose.   G. Saintsbury.

Gauckler, Ph.   Le Beau et son Histoire.   Paris: 1873.

Gayley, C. M., and F. N. Scott.   A Guide to the Literature of Aesthetics.   Univ. of Cal: 1890.

Genung, J. F.   The Practical Elements of Rhetoric.
Boston: 1887.   [2. 12. 3. 6.]

Gerber, G.   Die Sprache als Kunst.   2v.   Bromberg:
1871.   [3. 1. 1. 3.]

Gosse, E.   From Shakespeare to Pope.   Lond: 1885.
[2. 7. 4. 7.]

Gottschall, R.   Poetik.   3te. aufl. 2v. in 1.   Breslau: 1873.

Grabow, A.   Ueber Musik in der deutschen Sprache.
Lemgo: 1876.

Gray, Th.   Works in Prose and Verse.   Ed. by E.
Gosse.   4v.   Lond: 1884.   [2. 10. 1. 3.]

Grundriss der Germanischen Philologie.   Hrsg. von. H.
Paul.   1 Lief. Methodenlehre von H. Paul.   Strassburg:
1889.

Gummere, F. B.   A Handbook of Poetics.   Boston:
1885.   [2. 12. 1. 4.]

Gurney, Edm.   The Power of Sound.   Lond: 1880.
[3. 16. 4. 5.]

Guyau, Ch.   Les Problèmes de l'esthétique contemporaine.   Paris: 1884.

Hamilton, Sir Wm.   Lectures on Metaphysics and Logic.
2v.   Boston: 1860.   [3. 15. 1. 6.]

Hartmann, E. von.   Ausgewählte Werke.   2 Syst. Theil
der Aesthetik.   Berlin: 1887.   [3. 16. 1. 5.]

Hauptmann, M.   The Nature of Harmony and Metre.

Trans. and Ed. by W. E. Heathcote. N. Y: 1888. [3. 16. 4. 6.]

Hegel, G. W. F. Werke. 18v. Berlin: 1833–48. [3. 14. 5.. 7.] Bd. 10, Th. 1–3 Aesthetik.

Helmholtz, H. L. F. Sensations of Tone as a Psychological Basis for the Theory of Music. Trans. and Ed. by A. J. Ellis. Lond: 1875. [4. 5. 4. 7.]

Henry, Ch. Rapporteur Esthétique. Paris: 1888.

Higginson, T. W. Atlantic Essays. Boston: 1871. [2. 6. 5. 6.]

Hill, D. J. The Science of Rhetoric. N. Y: 1886. [2. 12. 3. 4.]

Hill, A. S. The Principles of Rhetoric and their Application. N. Y: 1878.

Hobbes, Th. English Works. Lond: 1840. [3. 14. 4. 5.]

Horace. Works. Trans. by C. Smart. Bohn ed. Lond: 1858. [3. 5. 1. 6.]

Hosmer, J. K. A Short History of German Literature. St. Louis: 1879. [3. 8. 2. 4.]

Hunt, T. W. Representative English Prose and Prose Writers. N. Y: 1887. [2. 7. 4. 7.]

Hunt, T. W. Studies in Literature and Style. N. Y: 1890. [2. 7. 4. 8.]

James, W. The Principles of Psychology. N. Y: 1890.

Johnson, S. Works. 11 v. Oxford: 1825. [2. 10. 1. 4.]

Jonson, Ben. Works. Ed. by Gifford. 9 v. Lond: 1875. [2. 14. 2. 7.]

Joubert, J. Pensées ... précédées d'une notice ... par P. de Raynal. 2 v. Paris: 1877–80. [3. 7. 2. 4.]

Kames, Lord. Elements of Criticism. N. Y: 1838. [2. 12. 3. 5.]

Kawczynski, M. Essai comparatif sur l'origine et l'histoire des rythmes. Paris: 1889.

Laurie, S. S. Lectures on Language and Linguistic Method in the School. Cambridge: 1890. [5. 6. 5. 5.]

Lessing, G. E. Selected Prose Works. Trans. by Beasley and Zimmern. Bohn ed. Lond: 1879. [3. 8. 5. 4.]

Lewes, G. H. The Principles of Success in Literature. Repr. by A. S. Cook. San Francisco: 1885. [2. 7. 3. 7.] [Same in Fortn. 1: 85, 185, 572, 697; 2: 257, 689.]

——— Problems of Life and Mind. 3d Ser. 2 v. Boston: 1879–80. [3. 15. 2. 5.]

Long, Geo. An Old Man's Thoughts about Many Things. 2d ed. Lond: 1872. [2. 6. 5. 7.]

Longinus, Dionysius. On the Sublime. Trans. from the Greek, with notes, by Wm. Smith. 5th ed. Lond: 1800. [2. 12. 3. 5.]

Longridge, C. C. The Formation of English Writers. 3d ed. 3 v. Lond. [2. 12. 3. 6].

Lord, D. N. Characteristics and Laws of Figurative Language. N. Y: 1854. [2. 12. 3. 5.]

Lotze, H. Microcosmus. Trans. by E. Hamilton and E. E. C. Jones. 2 v. Edinb.: 1885. [3. 15. 2. 3.]

Marmontel, J. F. Eléments de Littérature. 3v. Paris: 1846. [3. 7. 2. 2.]

Marsh, G. P. Lectures on the English Language. 1st Ser. 4th Ed. N. Y: 1863. [2. 12. 2. 4.]

Masson, D. Essays Biographical and Critical. Camb: 1856. [2. 7. 4. 5.]

Mayor, J. B. Chapters on English Metre. Lond: 1886. [2. 12. 1. 4.]

Minto, W. Manual of English Prose Literature. Boston: 1889. [2. 7. 3. 5.]

Mod. Lang. Asso. Pubs., Vol. 4, No. 1. Some Points in the Study of English Prose Style. H. E. Shepherd.

Mod. Lang. Notes. 3:29. Matter and Manner in Literary Composition. J. G. R. McElroy. [3. 10. 3. 1.]

—— 3:113. Macaulay and Carlyle. J. M. Hart.

—— 3:251. The Evolution of Figures of Speech. J. P. Fruit.

Morley, H., and Tyler, M. C. A Manual of English Literature. N. Y: 1880. [3. 7. 3. 4.]

Morley, J. On the Study of Literature. Lond: 1887. [2. 7. 4. 8.]

—— Voltaire. N. Y: 1872. [3. 7. 1. 4.]

Morley, H. English Writers. Lond: 1887. [2. 7. 3. 2.]

Mueller, Max. The Science of Thought. 2v. N. Y: 1887. [Catal. R.]

—— Three Introductory Lectures on the Science of Thought. Lond: 1888. [Catal. R.]

Nettleship, H. The Moral Influence of Literature: Classical Education in the Past and Present. Two Popular Addresses. Lond: 1890. [3. 4. 2. 2.]

Neue Jahrb. f. Philol. u. Paed. 135:681. Zur Geschichte der Stilarten. H. Liers.

—— 132:114. Die Gattungen der Prosa. Edm. Weissenborn.

Newman, J. H., Cardinal. The Idea of a University Defined and Illustrated. Lond: 1881. [5. 6. 5. 4.]

Pater, W. Appreciations; with an Essay on Style. Lond: 1889. [2. 7. 4. 7.] [Essay on Style also in Fortn. 50:728.]

Paul, H. Principles of the History of Language. Trans. fr. 2d ed. by H. A. Strong. N. Y: 1889. [3. 1. 1. 4.]

Peile, J.   Philology.   (Lit Primers.)   Lond: 1877.   [3.
1. 1. 6.]

Posnett, H. M.   Comparative Literature.   N. Y: 1886.
[2. 7. 1. 1.]

Puttenham, Geo.   The Arte of English Poesie.   Engl.
Reprints ... ed. by E. Arber.   Lond: 1869.   [2. 10. 5. 6.]

Quintilian.   The Institutes of Oratory.   Trans. by J. S.
Watson.   Bohn Libr.   2v.   Lond: 1882.   [3. 5. 4. 3.]

Renton, W.   The Logic of Style, being an Introduction
to Critical Science.   Lond: 1874.   [2. 12. 3. 4.]

Rev. Philos.   22:1.   De la Parole et des sons intérieurs.
Stricker.

——— 28:356.   Le Contraste, le Rythme, la Mesure.
Ch. Henry.

Richter, Jean Paul.   Vorschule der Aesthetik.   3v.
Stuttgart: 1813.   [3. 16. 1. 5.]

Royal Irish Acad.   Trans.   v. 5.   p. 39–92.   R. Burrowes.   On Style in Writing.   [4. 1. 3.]

Ruskin, J.   Elements of English Prosody.   Orpington:
1880.

——— Modern Painters.   5v.   Orpington: 1887.   [3.
17. 3. 4.]

——— On the Old Road.   3v.   Orpington: 1885.   [3.
17. 3. 2.]   Vol. 2 Fiction, Fair and Foul.   Esp. p. 88.
Same in 19th C. 8:401.

Sainte-Beuve, C. A.   Causeries de Lundi.   3e ed.   15v.
Paris: 1857–62.   [3. 7. 5. 2.]

Saintsbury, G. W.   Specimens of English Prose Style
...with an Introductory Essay.   London: 1884.   [2. 7.
1. 6.]

Scherr, Joh.   Allgemeine Geschichte der Literatur.   2v.
Stuttgart: 1881–82.   [Dorsch L.]

Schipper, J. Euglische Metrik. 2v. Bonn: 1881–88. [2. 12. 1. 4.]

Schmidt, J. H. H. Introduction to the Rhythmic and Metric of the Classical Languages. Trans. by J. W. White. Boston: 1878. [3. 2. 1. 7.]

Schopenhauer, A. Sämmtliche Werke. 6v. Leipzig: 1877. [3. 15. 1. 5.]

—— The World as Will and Idea. Trans. by R. B. Haldane and J. Kemp. 3v. Lond: 1883. [3. 15. 1. 5.]

Shairp, J. C. Aspects of Poetry. Boston: 1882. [2. 8. 1. 7.]

Sidney, Sir Ph. An Apologie for Poetrie. Engl. Reprints ... ed. by E. Arber. Lond: 1868. [2. 10. 5. 6.]

Spencer, Herbert. First Principles. Lond: 1862. [3. 15. 2. 6.]

—— Essays: Moral, Political and Aesthetic. N. Y: 1873. [3. 15. 2. 6.] Essay on Style.

Spengel, L. Ueber das Studium der Rhetorik bei den Alten. Muenchen: 1842. [2. 12. 3. 4.]

Stael, Mme. de. De la Littérature. Paris: 1845. [3. 7. 2. 5.]

Stedman, E. C. Poets of America. Boston: 1885. [2. 7. 4. 7.]

—— Victorian Poets. Boston: 1879. [2. 7. 4. 7.]

Stephen, L. Hours in a Library. Ser. 1–3. [2. 7. 4. 7.]

Stevenson, R. L. See Contemp.

Sully, Jas. Outlines of Psychology. Lond: 1884. [3. 15. 4. 1.]

Swinburne, A. C. Essays and Studies. Lond: 1875. [2. 7. 5. 6.]

Sylvester, J. J. The Laws of Verse. Lond: 1870. [2. 12. 1. 4.]

Symonds, J. A. Sketches and Studies in Italy. Lond: 1879. [3. 16. 1. 6.]

Taine, H. A. History of English Literature. Trans. by H. Van Laun. Lond: 1883. 3v. [2. 7. 3. 4.]

Thirlwall, C., Bishop. Essays, Speeches and Sermons. Ed. by J. J. S. Perowne. Lond: 1880. [1. 8. 3. 5.]

Venables, E. John Bunyan. Great Writers Series. Lond: 1888. [2. 10. 3. 4.]

Viehoff, H. Die Poetik auf. d. Grundlage d. Erfahrungsseelenlehre. Trier: 1888.

Vinet, Alex. Outlines of Philosophy and Literature. 2d ed. Lond: 1867. [3. 15. 3. 7.]

Vischer, F. T. Aesthetik oder Wissenschaft des Schönen. 3v. Reutlingen: 1846. [3. 16. 1. 5.]

Volkmann, R. Die Rhetorik der Griechen und Römer. Berlin: 1872. [2. 12. 3. 5.]

Voltaire, F. M. A. de. Oeuvres Complètes. 50v. Paris: 1877–83. [3. 7. 1.]

Wackernagel, W. Poetik, Rhetorik und Stilistik. Halle: 1873.

Walter, E. L. Lessing on the Boundaries of Poetry and Painting. Ann Arbor: 1888. [3. 8. 5. 4.]

Warner, C. D. Washington Irving. Am. Men of Letters Series. Boston: 1882. [2. 9. 2. 2.]

. Webbe, Wm. A Discourse of English Poetrie. Engl. Reprints ... ed. by E. Arber. Lond: 1870. [2. 10. 5. 6.]

Weil, H. The Order of Words in the Ancient Languages compared with that of the Modern Languages. Trans. by C. W. Super. Boston: 1887.

Whitney, W. D. Language and the Study of Language. N. Y: 1867. [3. 1. 1. 5.]

——— Life and Growth of Language. N. Y: 1877. [3. 1. 1. 4.]

Zeitsch. f. Völkerpsychologie. 4:465. Zur Stylistik. H. Steinthal.

——— 6:285. Poesie und Prosa. H. Steinthal.